The Long Red Coat

Written by
Jill Atkins

Illustrated by
Carmen Sanchez

Ransom

Shem had ten chickens.

Zak had a foal.

Beth had Gosh, the goat.

Gosh was a big, bad goat!

Beth had a long red coat.

At night Beth hung the long red coat on a peg.

The peg was high up in the shed.

At night Shem fed the chickens
and Zak fed the foal.

Gosh the goat was in his pen.

His pen was in the shed.

Beth ran to the shed.

She ran to get the long red coat.

But Beth had a shock.

The coat was not on the high peg.

The coat was not in the shed.

Beth ran up to Gosh the goat.

In the light, Gosh was a sight!

He had red bits on his chin.

It was the long red coat!

Gosh the goat had fed on the coat.

Gosh the goat was a big, bad goat!